Whispers from the Aural World

Karolyn Redoute

Whispers from the Aural World

Karolyn Redoute

Plain View Press, LLC
1101 W 34th Street, STE 404

www.plainviewpress.net
Austin, TX 78705

Copyright © 2018 Karolyn Redoute All rights reserved under International and Pan-American Copyright Conventions. No part of this book may be reproduced or distributed in any form or by any means, or stored in a data base or retrieval system, without written permission from the author. All rights, including electronic, are reserved by the author and publisher.

ISBN: 978-1-63210-034-4
Library of Congress Control Number: 2018933280

Cover image: *The Difference Between Hearing and Listening* by Angela Kallsen
Interior art: *Ready Wings* by Amy Egenberger
Author photo by Greg Steinke
Cover design by Pam Knight

We Find Healing In Existing Reality
Plain View Press is a 36-year-old issue-based literary publishing house. Our books result from artistic collaboration between writers, artists, and editors. Over the years we have become a far-flung community of humane and highly creative activists whose energies bring humanitarian enlightenment and hope to individuals and communities grappling with the major issues of our time—peace, justice, the environment, education and gender.

for Joan Penrose

a light in our lives

Acknowledgements
Gratitude to these publications for prior printing of these poems:
- "Confessions" in *Earth Daughters* (Fall 2011).
- "To A Woman Somewhere on the Autism Spectrum" in *Slant: A Journal of Poetry* (Summer 2017).

My thanks to Sherry Quan Lee for her help in editing this manuscript.

Contents

I Darkness and Light	**15**
Sanctuary	17
A Lesson on Time	18
Mystery and Melancholy of a Street	19
Apprehension	20
The Origins of Fear	21
Father Framed in a Doorway	22
Confessions	23
The Words of the Astrologer	25
Dream of a Glass House	27
House Burning	29
Detroit: The Prophetic Street	30
Woman on a Porch in Detroit, 2002	33
Detroit's East Side, 2016	34
Invisible Mirrors	36
II Silence and Sound	**39**
Voices	41
Assembling the Heart	42
Birth	43
Whispers from the Aural World	44
To a Woman Somewhere on the Autism Spectrum	45
Woman at the Window	46
The Art of Understanding a Woman in a Shell	47
Listening to a Memory	48
Hearing the Truth	50
The Listener	51
The Moon's Face	52
The Carpenter's Question	53
Vespers	55
All Things of the Body, A River	56
Aerial Vanitas	57
Sky in Late Summer	58
Buried Shadows	59

III Healing and Dreams	**63**
Awakening	65
The Poet Imprisoned	66
As If in Blessing	67
Light	68
Forever, St. Valentine	69
The Fate of Cheap Mirrors	70
Four Thoughts About a Ladder	71
Vigil	72
Solace	74
Venus Amoris	75
Vesica Pisces: What Could Be	77
About the Author	79

"The whisper of the word in the unseen
is the music of meaning made new..."

Mahmoud Darwish, A *River Dies of Thirst*

1 Darkness and Light

Sanctuary

The games of hide and seek had ended
under the street lamps, and I came inside
to the darkened house. My mother sat
in the armchair in the corner, not speaking

as she said her prayers. I could hear
the iridescent glass beads of the rosary
moving between her narrow fingers,
rubbing like small crystals spread by hand

around a candle. She didn't gaze on illumined
books of hours, or rose windows in the darkness
of the living room. Instead, after finishing
the beads, she moved to the porch, unaware

that stars take light years to travel
to our sight, and by the time of their arrival,
no longer represent their origin in the sky.
She prayed to that eternity anyway,

as if it offered all of us salvation.
If she prayed for me, as I am sure
she did, it is hard for me to know
if her prayers were ever answered.

A Lesson on Time

"There is no time in heaven,"
my mother happened to say
one day when we were children
pretending to be angels

in the hallway. "There are no
relationships in heaven." I would guess
she meant no passion, drama
or longing; but perhaps I read that

somewhere, and that isn't what
she meant at all, and I am now mistaken
that she said that much. It was just
an ordinary afternoon.

She was sweeping the kitchen.
My sister and I were playing
in the hallway. The teakettle was
whistling. It was almost summer.

Mystery and Melancholy of a Street

In the twilight I see
the street beyond the sun-
soaked walls, near
an archway of stone.

A girl with flowing hair
turns a hoop with a stick
beyond the railway
and the industry of town.

I cannot know
if she ever lived to see
beyond the mystery
of time and

the melancholy stone,
that place where
we all wait
in the hours between

evening and night,
and night and day,
more in shadow
than in light.

She moves with grace
and yet is still.
Time stops
as I look at her,

and turn away,
aware of the lost
astrology
of evening,

of all she will
know, and will
never know,
in the years ahead.

Apprehension

She flew at night to find her children's fears,
spotting blue and yellow balls on streets,
tricycles lying sideways on the lawn,
and dolls thrown upon the neighbor's roof.

Most nights, though, she failed to locate any traces
of her daughters' fear. As they grew,
she flew more often, late at night, above cross
walks, fences, street lamps and fire hydrants,

searching wildly in the dark, but too often,
to no avail. Then she decided to fly deeper,
even later in the night, descending down
to storefronts, knocking on the shuttered doors,

in case some neighbor girl had been abandoned
there. After flying over alleyways and roads,
she would come home early in the morning,
empty-handed, in regret. In time she realized

her greatest fears concerned her husband,
who would, like her, stay up till the early
morning hours. She was alarmed to find
that he was drinking gin, steering the house

as if it were a car, clutching a map, trying to find
out where she went. Meanwhile, their daughters
stirred, at times, with nightmares in the dark,
in what seemed an empty house.

The Origins of Fear

As a young women, I had a dream
of a beast running after me,
in my neighborhood. It was summer.
This beast pursued me, street

after street. In the dream, I ran away
on crutches, never seeking asylum
in any of the houses, never stopping,
lest I be killed, or else, ravaged

to my womb. It was a girl's unspoken
fear of life, perhaps of love. The dream
only happened once, but for many years,
I could not trace its origins

to any single being. If it was imaginary,
a yeti, for example, it did not speak
of its intentions in writing, or reveal itself
in bestiaries, or through other books.

It simply did not show itself. And so,
I kept running as the victim, never
believing I would win the race to be,
or to be loved. But now in returning

to the ruined houses of that street,
the beast I see is more like a man
forced to live in a suit he didn't want,
forced to swim within the skin of a shadow

he could not contain. I see he is running past me;
he is, in fact, my fear of him. I can't ask
him to restore the life I lost in his pursuit, or
to save me from my flight.

Father Framed in a Doorway

In each season he would stand there, at least once,
feeling no solace, in staying or going, still as a bell
that could not move back and forth,
that was my father. The back of his head was as dark
as the streets of a war-torn city,
his legs apart, like a soldier
at ease, but not at ease. His body waited,
unsure at the gates of the squadron, afraid, silenced;

and so, his stories waited with him, at the threshold,
at the doorway no one could cross.

Confessions

A square door in the chimney.
There my father lit small fires
in the basement, stoking flames
like a midshipman while we slept.

Past midnight, he wrote letters
to the missionary fathers
about his faith in God.
Waking once, I heard his steps

pounding the basement floor,
the clink of glass in the metal
can, a cap falling off another
Stroh's, into the quiet dark.

After I left home, I forgot
about my father's nights
and all his correspondence.
When I traveled to Hawaii

and the blue Pacific,
I saw him at last as he was:
an old sailor dragging
his iron shoes toward

the darkened stairs,
a man marooned
in sand, and injured
by the dark. I smelled oil fires

in the sea and felt the heat
of burning palms, under
an ashen moon;
and I imagined more.

Yet whatever my father wrote,
he wrote in secret. I believe
the drunken pages
of his letters

were often burned
by morning to cool ash,
and his confessions
never mailed.

The Words of the Astrologer

Her office was in an attic where an illumined
globe showed each constellation.

I could touch the warm stars that night,
as if reading my fate in braille.

I was listening in the dark. The night showed
through a skylight. She carefully told me

I had been born *under a grand cross*.
I think of this whenever I see leaves

flow backward in daylight,
how they are pulled in all

directions, though they are rooted
to a tree in the earth, and how

they go in and out of calm, at the wind's
calling, just before a storm.

Yet, if I looked up at the night sky,
I would be unable to identify the tension

of the stars that pulled me once
like a strained rope offered to the lost.

Ten years later, the second astrologer said,
You have the natal chart of a child

of prison camp parents, again, the blue print
of sorrow fixed by my birth. Neither reader

had witnessed my sister and I, in early photos
in our youth, looking thin to the bone,

like survivors of our parent's early lives.
Neither had heard stories about early death

from my mother, or how my sister and I
bore in our anatomy the stories of war

my father never told. There was no guide book
given. Only the path of the stars.

Dream of a Glass House

Under an early moon in April
a small house of glass in mist,
in an empty field.
The house is mine.

I recognize the roof, silver
like the sky, and
three walls of glass.
The fourth wall is now

deeply green wild
grass moving inward
toward the house.
I approach.

Only now can I hear
rushing waves on
the distant shore.
Wind is blowing the tall

grass into the house
from the sea. There is no door.
I must move through
as if crossing high water,

even if it means I drown
in wind; when the storm
has passed from my body,
it is nearly night.

My arms are shaking.
I see the house is empty,
and there is no hearth,
though I can't say I was expecting

any, or love or peace. Inside
the house is as black as old iron,
as if it had been on fire
once, and then abandoned.

I hear murmurs of water
falling down the spiral staircase
into the center of the house,
distantly at first,

then, like a child laughing, the sound
brims over each step
into a stream.
I look up through the dark

shingles of the roof, now blue
with night, to a round hole
the water is falling from,
my eyes are infinite with light,

moonlight,

and I realize I didn't know
myself when I lived
in the house, or how long
I had been walking toward it

and how, as much as I have tried,
I cannot save it
from the grass,
nor is there any time.

House Burning

The stone steps wait
until no one remembers their purpose.

Detroit: The Prophetic Street

I
It is too late to board the arc
to form a covenant.
The exodus never intended
to save the houses

left behind, properties
forsaken by the prophecies
of real estate agents
and banks.

II
The doors have fallen
away with their stories
into the fires
of vandals, who take

shelter in abandoned
living rooms. The windows
are boarded. Some trembling
burnt laths, once walls,

fall against each other
shaking like ladders.
Each house waits to step
down into flames.

III
On our old street birds fly
from twisted rafters where
you can see the sky. The houses
come apart slat by slat, wall by wall.

Birds emerge in all directions
trying to fly upward,
as if every day is the day
after a storm: a storm

of wind, or else of rain,
or fire. This pattern repeats,
day after day, night
after night, for miles.

    IV
A bird lights on a wire
above the small brick house
of the man who walked
our street talking to himself.

Where is he now, I wonder?
Like him, the street is a tightrope
walker who has thrown away
the balancing pole from above.

The street is a false prophet,
who walks the water of heaven,
but sinks into the grassy earth,
cowering, afraid.

    V
The city discards the clothes
it no longer needs from a suitcase,
like a refugee. It waits
for whatever happens next.

There is no boat scheduled.
The train, like the depot,
has been gone many years.
No city services, no lights.

    VI
Now, on my broken street,
I am a refugee too, trying to
balance a memory, going back
with a vacant map

to the narrow hallway
of the small A-frame house
sided in asbestos, its small
rooms and square yard;

three blocks away, the school
still stands, and the church
where I first heard the bells
across the city field,

as if it was a hundred
miles of open land
from our house,
as if it crossed a river

and endless blue tributaries,
the river roads I dreamed
of leaving on. Our house will
be gone soon, taken down

to the ground, and I will
lose the continuity
of its story in my mind.
Like others in my generation,

I rode away before
the coming storm,
just as the messages
of hate and lies caused

the neighborhoods to fulfill
a prophecy they had expected
to come true. I mean the flight
of fear, flight as white as fear.

Woman on a Porch in Detroit, 2002

The street shakes, trembles as if held
at gunpoint. It is summer, an afternoon
losing light in the clouds.

It is hard for anyone to rest his or her
eyes. The sidewalks are deserted.
There are no dreams at doorways,

or welcomes at thresholds, no one
returns with a gift, or walks a dog,
or comes home from a job.

The street is empty, except for
an older woman sitting on a porch,
a three-year old sprawled across

her lap. Two adolescent boys sit next
to her on chairs. The closed front door
is to her left. She is gazing out past

the house, as if the rescuers arrived
too late, her eyes riveted on the blank
horizon stretching over the broken

roofs. As I am looking at her,
she and the young boys in faded
clothes are staring past our car.

They do not seem to see us.
But then, in the moments we enter
this street, we all become ghosts,

like survivors of an accident,
the light around our bodies stunned.
It has been years since I looked

into her eyes looking past mine,
years since I remember feeling
like an apparition in the midday heat.

Detroit's East Side, 2016

My sister steers the Ford Fusion. We hurry down
the asphalt street, to our old house on the corner.
It used to be green, but the siding
has changed to the blanched
color of smoke,

as if the house
had become a nameless cloud.
Tracks of soot, like handprints, trail
from the blue- boarded attic
window, and all the other
windows, as if you could
nail plywood
to the sky.

Seeing the signs
in the empty silence,
my sister and I

now become
part of the landscape
in-between pale smoke
and fire,
ourselves fading
to ash,

then we see
our small corner lot barren
of the chain link
fence, the plum tree,
the river rock, along its edge.
The old markers no longer
there,

we become transported
into air, lose gravity, and time.
My sister tries to pause the car

as we pass our old garage,
open, now, without its door.

Someone is living there homeless.

There is a hill of trash in the alley
smelling of honeysuckle.

My sister and I then move
very fast in the car. The few trees
look like startled children,
as we drive away to the next street,
and the next, and the next,
and the next.

Invisible Mirrors

In our small house, there were no expansive rooms
where mirrors could offer knowledge. Such mirrors

are expensive, and difficult to place on walls,
and require the understanding of the art

of prophecy and eternal truth. There are
less elaborate mirrors, too, that welcome

questions. My father and mother desperately
needed one of these to offer counsel,

time, advice or silence, as an invitation
to reflect. They didn't know they had a choice.

Rather, they looked away while arguing
in the living room where a mirror

might have helped them most. They bore
their hurt, letting any glance, or offer

of conciliation, or consolation, pass.
And so the arguments continued. Those words

echoing into all the rooms, those unresolved
anxieties, never counseled, would be left for me

to carry after I left home. I took my reflections
from the walls and fled without suspecting.

But then one day, when I re-discovered them,
I saw I had no mirrors, either, only glass

that had broken into shards. I tried to force
the pieces into focus, but it would take years

for me to find my own reflection, to hear
the questions my parents never asked.

11 Silence and Sound

Hearing the Truth

You are like someone standing in a doorway
who didn't hear at first.

And then suddenly, with the news,
your eyes turn to milk (a milky blue),
your hands tremble,
and you seem to become
someone else.

Life is a disorderly journey,
sometimes a journey
you hadn't intended.
The face can change, but also
the body, at sudden news,
and of course, the eyes:

one eye, eclipsed, quiet,
holds still like the moon, taking in the shadows;
the other eye, like a sphere in transit,
becomes a ghost.

The eye is a ghost,
then. The ghost is a child

drowning in the sea,
twice, once on a storm-crossed shore,
once now.

Voices

Voices, come
to me imagined
half in this world,
half in another,
and what am I
but a messenger.

Assembling the Heart

I didn't know that over time, my heart had become invisible,
to anyone who came close enough to hear it beating.
My face no longer informed people of the truth, and love
became an awkward art. For a long time I believed

this problem was rooted elsewhere in my body. I visited
various practitioners who I believed could cure me of
my maladies. I tried to recover on my own, as the shame of being
unloved, or loved mistakenly, is great, but then I realized

that my unread heart had indeed become so silent, it was almost
unresponsive. Eventually, I was referred to someone
who could hold my heart in suspension, so that I could try
to unlock each piece that, over the years, had been jammed

into working. When I did, at once, the pieces fell like windows
from a shaken house, without a trace of the pattern
from the childhood I remembered. I continued on, even so,
with my make-shift self, not being who I thought I was,

but believing that, if I re-assembled each piece, and learned
the path of my feelings, one day my life would become
a work of art. Without this illusion, the illusion of life as art,
without my naïve belief, I would not have continued,

and would not be writing now. Of course, it takes a lifetime
to re-assemble such an intricate timepiece as the heart,
and often the work is never finished. I know this now.

Birth

I never learned to swim.

I floundered from the womb
and held my breath and
believed I could,

and closed my eyes

to the rushing in the shallows,
the rhythm of the air,
the lulling sound of words,

and then I entered....

Whispers from the Aural World

When I was very young, we walked below an infinite
sky at noon, along the cresting waves....

The ear is a shell, an ocean calling, of holding and loss,
holding and loss. Shell to ear, ear to shell, circumaural,
we stood listening to the waves. The labyrinth
of my silence as a child fell into the chambers of the shell;
the winding talk between you and me, the beating of my child's
arrhythmic heart brought the pounding ocean to my ear through
the shell. We continued along the threshold of sound,
winding and curving along the shore, as we tuned
to the waves, their twisting and curving, winding and falling,
through your heart to mine.

The ear is the entrance to life, the long curving of its pearl
a passage you must take, through sorrow, through joy.
The long sandy beach we continued to walk,
like mother and child, entering the place
between hearing and the sentient world,
and *the heart of love:*

you must learn through a lifetime
to listen, and hope you can survive the rushing
sea, bring all of yourself to belief, and hope
the long curving beach you walk comes back
to you at last in
the whisper of beginnings, hear them,
go on, in spite of loss....

And now,
though you can no longer hear, I see there is still a threshold
of light between us, two ovals of a soul-shell,
from that day: sand and water, silence and sound,
end and beginning, life and death,
you and me.

To a Woman Somewhere on the Autism Spectrum

Consider, the days of St. George, maiden and dragon,
the beast, who hides in a cave, and the woman
who needs saving, the town indifferent to both;
the story, very worn, that no one now believes.

But it comes to life, as a story, when I think of you,
your nervous presence, so like a beast,
and a maiden held in ransom, at the same time.
I have noticed that you can't speak when you try,

the words gag in your throat, you become mute.
Without a saint to rescue you, no words come,
people ignore you, and despair of the conversation
that never comes. You are used to silence

and waiting in expressionless distress, and watch
while the person waiting for a reply loses patience,
and leaves. Who is ever good at rescue, or at flight?
Another time, earlier, when I approached you,

you tried to be grounded like a prey animal,
with a heart on fire holding the fire in,
and then you turned toward me
and the sound of an insult came out,

perhaps unintended, your voice faded
like the rearing dragon wounded in its cave.
And I too, withdrew, like the others.
And so the next time we were in the same

public space, I saw you looking down, tending
the dragon's hearth, keeping close to the invisible
fire you hold within, avoiding me. Could you ever
wish for a miracle, a vision of an orange tree

whose nectar would bring you to life
as a being calm and at ease, whose words
of love could flow? Could you embrace
the maiden in your heart, or let the dragon go?

Woman at the Window

It is as if you are blind, deaf and mute, and yet,
none of these. You are in a shell like a memory
of the sea in winter, where there is no sea.
Speak to me, then, in silence, your shell unfurling,

but still. I can only listen. You freeze
in place, when anyone approaches;
whatever beauty is in you freezes too.
Beauty truly then becomes the art

of camouflage. You have mastered the art
of being white in the darkness of your flight.
What you think is elusive, untraceable,
without the essence of speech. Now you are

like the winter moon moving across the sky,
expressionless. The moon's face at night
is caught in space, and hangs in another dimension,
is there, yet not there, in the blue exterior

silence. It is you I seek, but don't seek, since
I know better than to try. Wearied, I lose interest
in questioning the moon and where
it takes any of us each night, and turn

away from the wide window in the living
room in a kind of surrender. Your face resembles
this landscape, lost: a memory, a scene,
a frozen beach I can no longer place. You could

be any place, moment, person.
I would seek you, and never find you
as long as I looked,
though you are there.

The Art of Understanding a Woman in a Shell

You make one mistake in what you whisper
into her ear, as she leans toward you,
as she takes the incredible chance
to hear you as the band plays.

Even though you are nervous, you manage to make
some offhand comment about the music.
It won't take her long to believe she is mistaken:
you've no wish to be friends at all. You might

wave to someone else, just then, turning away
for a second and when you look back, you see
she has disappeared. You can almost see
the outline of her body, her energy go up in smoke,

like the smoke after a gun goes off,
when the air is bitter and acrid with regret.
But there is nothing you can do about the air.
You've no mutual friends. It will take you months

of watching her go the other direction on the street
to question whether you have been taken for a bully.
Those neighbors that she knows stare at you,
avoiding you, as if you were a thief.

And you know then you have entered a world
rather clumsily in which you do not know the rules.
Have you utterly failed at the art of understanding,
of realizing how easy it is for her to misunderstand

a word? A gesture, anything? So what value now is
your hesitant mind, and on paper, your metaphors, allusions,
symbols, allegories, and indirect ideas? Then again,
maybe it was not that way at all. Maybe you've only a theory

of how it was. But you see how you hide like her,
afraid of taking initiative, unsure, in social interaction,
and yet you know the so-called rules, and could easily
have risked the world, the world she risked for you.

Listening to a Memory

Seaside town. The Blue Line Road.
Sea and sky, legend
of brilliant light at noon,
and fading light
at end of day.
I am a child.

My mother is driving
back from town. I stand up
in the back seat and see
the steering wheel turn and lock
in her hands before the blue
ghost of the gravel road.

I hunch down, as she tells me,
hiding from the woman
I am too young to really know.
The car swerves and hits
the spreading ash tree.
The car rotates twice

in the blue dust.
I am the clothes
in the dark gas dryer,
the gray mouse running
in her golden cage, the turtle
hiding in the dark

green shell. In the fields
the tobacco pickers
in bandanas rush toward us
like a sea of silent, phantom
birds. The man behind us
draws my mother out

of the driver's door,
then me, through the blue
window I roll down.
I am turned, and turned, and turned
into the blue breath
of a new, and shaken

world. My mother and I
survive the afternoon,
and then the night.
How we spoke
in days ahead,
I am unsure.

The Listener

As a child, I looked into the glass eyes of a saint
in the darkened corner of a chapel, or into a prayer book
of icy words. Unused to staring back at the smooth glass
young girls comb their hair to see, I saw instead distortions,

from which I often ran. I stayed away from looking back,
but by the time I tried again, I was like a woman
with a stricken tongue who needed to relearn
the ways of speech. Barely able to hear the sound

of my own tears, I pounded the mirror, hoping
the broken sound would drown my child- like voice.
But the mirror didn't break. And I had to stand up
and go on, seeing into the sound. Exhausted

for years in my isolation, one day l relented,
like a prisoner of war, and let the mirror speak, though
still anxious from the relentless memories that it offered.
It was only because you were there that I began

to hear the words pounding within my heart in the icy
silence: the voice, rocking, as if a cold storm within,
as if it was myself, and only after many years
of your hearing did I look into *my* eyes, and heal.

The Moon's Face

The moon's face is
wounded, pock-marked
like a vagabond.

It comes and goes,
asking for coins,
and in the silence
just before
daybreak,
you have none.

The moon
continues to believe
in your goodness.

The Carpenter's Question

In memory of J. T. J.

Facing east, above the upstairs windows,
the arched stained glass, a clear sunburst rising
out of a mauve and green fleur-de-lis,
would have welcomed the morning.
At some point it was removed.
You can see the outline of its absence
in the yellow stucco.

I can put it back for you, the carpenter told me, as if
it had always been at the back of his mind, like the sun
on the lake. Then he left that afternoon
to go sailing.

The window hung in space.

In the time in- between, I worried
if the window would have a nail flange
or a proper membrane, if
in the end, it would leak like the rest
of the house. I worried about the slope
of the sill, the veins of splitting stucco.

When you hang a window

into empty space, to make it look out
of your eyes, and another's, you need a level,
to see if it is placed correctly, to see if it is
right and true, on either side,
and in this case, perhaps, a map

of the stars and sunrays far beyond
the stratosphere.

The window is still wrapped in darkness
in muslin cloth in the attic,
and the carpenter continues to sail
forever on the lake
into an eternity
of moonlight,
which was his dream.

Now I can only imagine him on the other side
floating in light. I would have remembered him
each time I returned home from work, as I looked up
at a setting sun, with its flowering rays, shifting
into shadow,

or at night, now,
if I looked up at a half moon shifting
into another moon, like a mandorla
in the time in- between
his asking and my hesitation
to hear.

Vespers

The carpenter would come, and go
making repairs. He told me once he liked
surprises. He left four small copper trays
on a window sill, out of nowhere,
like small spinnakers in procession
without rudder, or pole.

Then I did not hear from him,
and learned of his illness by chance.
The men at the lumberyard spoke
softly, unsure if they could share
his secret; he kept it from most
everyone. I sent flowers then,

too late. Within months, his widow
sent back the key to my house.
She could not give back the time
he spent on boats... *along
the shore in spring, she finds
row boats turned downward,*

*with their history of fear
secret in the transom,
the keel, the breasthook,
the curving gunwhale,
the bottomboards
held by the ribbing...*
and nothing consoles.

It is instead *the sails
in summer that bring peace
on the quiet beach: the main sails
full, the jibs full, the heads tilting
forward on the wind, measured,
patient, gliding, holding yet giving*

*breath, bringing the deep light forward
with the hastening wind, the last light
toward prayer.*

All Things of the Body, A River

The lake he sailed became a river,
almost overnight. Now he found
he could watch the stars, but not run
with them over the waves.
In his body the wood slats of his boat rolled
into the center of his being, his arms
and his boat became a dreamscape with lines
he could no longer grasp. The handling
of the ropes, the veering of the starboard side
had to become meditations of a shifting
journey. His legs became heavy
like a wooden craft that must wait
in silent harbor. In his eyes the measure
of the heavens became the distance
between him and what was left of his life.
He must have asked the sky
for reasons through long,
and useless, nights.

I only know the carpenter
read philosophies
about the art of living,
and the art of dying,
according to his daughter
at his service.

Death is like a birth,
said Marcus Aurelius,
a mystery of nature: the path
of a river, the end in the beginning,
the question held
in starlight.

Aerial Vanitas

From the air the exclusive subdivision:
pools of exquisite aqua, imitations of the sea
silent sand-colored, shingled mansion, its tiled roof the color
of dried blood glinting in the sun, I imagine

the wine glass fallen in the wind.
On the table next to the beach chair, barely visible but there,
a woven embroidered golden silk shawl has fallen across the chair
where a woman visitor sat staring at the sky

the night before. The clouds are the hourglass sands,
passing quickly now. The open, blue-lettered book rests, its pages lightly
moving on the chair, above the binding, impossible to see,
some poetry, some depth of the heart, some deep knowledge

abandoned there. The forest, on fire a year ago,
rises stiffly in the foothills, and from the air, the haze resembles smoke.
Nearby, no sound of bees, no hint of flowers, while skulls of small
creatures blackened in the crevices of trees tumble into earth.

The purple orchids, soft like pale paper, have fallen from an enamel vase,
fallen on another table near another chair, from last night's
party, the petals float in the blue
water in the pool, forgotten.

None of this nuance is visible from the air, no symbols
of transience, just one house, its anxieties and joys
extinguish, with the distance,
from the air.

Sky in Late Summer

In summer, Venus, the evening star, may seem elusive
as it languishes in the fire of a setting sun, and the red
Eye of Taurus, too, as it hides, but the moon
has a sense of eternity because of its infinite gaze,

which we return. The moon appears to be
without need, like an understanding landscape,
and then, may startle, just as easily,
like an apparition, or change into blue or blood.

But when its shadow passes like an illness, the moon
is whole again, beneficent. It bathes the porch
floor boards in pearls of light. I sit there on the rocker
in late August, and time passes till it is very late.

I know I have things to do, and that I will not do them
in time, and the moon will wait to hold my eyes
in its light as the sky changes and the land,
like all of us, turns inward.

Buried Shadows

The April ground beyond
the pond is pale with straw
and hollow stalks rise up
from a mound like long thin horns.
You can see in your mind
the outline of the beast below the ground,
standing there waiting to emerge.

The stalks turn green and the beast shakes
from its long sleep. We are shadows buried
below the horizon, waiting,
believing there will always be
an emergence of light
each year, that the buried beast
will bow into its being
and will wake and
walk the earth.

III Healing and Dreams

Awakening

When I hear chimes in the yard,
I think of you. There is a wise man
in the East who does not think
at all when he hears
chimes floating over the mountain.
I wish I could empty my mind
like him, like the wind in the range,
and live in the mountains
far away from this house
and be one with empty trees.

The Poet Imprisoned

And when they come for me by name, tell them
to read the golden stars in the center
of the white flowers, where I hid my heart
in the cherry blossoms, for safe keeping.

Say how I left the words there for nearly
a century, petals unfurling with a wisdom
I could almost know, lost when I was forced
into hiding. Do not decode the words exactly,

as you may miss the meaning of the letters
in your determination to transform them; think
instead of my phrases as clouds passing. Keep
the rhythm of the soft unclothing

of blossoms in your heart and believe in it,
as you would your love, and drink
in the scent of her, even if you hardly
understand the meaning anymore of her gaze;

they will not steal them then, or destroy them.
Or when I am hidden like a hooded
figure in a vast desert, when you cannot seek
the words I am saying, during wartime,

because the words are blackened,
and all you hear is stammering
in another language, follow me
in your mind's eye, alone, and go with me,

though I am invisible, disguised, hard
to trust, even parted from my true mind,
imprisoned by flailing dust; if by some
miracle you can see my truth

in a dream this way, even for a moment,
and though I disappear at times from your
sight in the future, believe in me still,
as you would the cherry blossoms.

Karolyn Redoute

As If in Blessing

Early spring, patches of snow in a field.
Oaks and tall green firs in the mist.
In the clearing a man turns

and lets go of a hawk
from the palm of his gloved hand,
his arms raised, as if

in blessing. The hawk's talons
are tied to a tether,
held by another man.

The hawk is still unable to fly skyward
into the trees. Walking toward
the grounded hawk, the man

with the gloved hands looks
toward the clearing, his movements
slow, and patient, like prayer;

and the man with the tether
looks toward the clouds with hope,
his eyes cast, like a falconer,

onto the blue world,
medieval and hallowed, when birds
were hunters, but also souls,

lost or otherwise, looking
for home. There is an ancestral
memory of hope in the eyes

of both men, a spreading,
then a falling away,
of wings, each morning,

as the hawk calls to them,
holding them in place
and time.

Light

I wake a child,
calling as softly
as mist rising
from the shore,
hoping to offer
her light.

Forever, St. Valentine

I remember praying for love when I was young.
I believe I needed a miracle, so fervent

was my request for intercession. Asking for
divine intervention is a sign of desperation,

but I had begun to take imploring for granted.
That is when I began to believe in love

from a distance. It was safer there, trying
to lasso the moon from a juniper tree

in the desert, or attempting to call off
daybreak over the ocean from the shore.

When prayer failed me in the way I expected,
I imagined wild places where I could fall in love.

This lead me to stand amid the everlasting
flowers in my early thirties on the white cliffs.

I found myself believing in *forever*, there, and again
in the mountains deep with rhododendron in spring;

swaying on the buoyant wooden bridge, I felt the rain
fall gently on both of us, thinking:

this will be forever. Instead, I would learn
in years to come about the nature of rain,

its stormy, unpredictable thunder, how it toys
with the sun and the clouds, and comes and goes,

often without asking, how it mimics the insistent
rhythm of a child's hopeless prayer

to a phantom saint, the way it falls away
like legend, and then becomes myth.

The Fate of Cheap Mirrors

When the mirror was new, it searched for shards of our being:
shiny blue and green bottle glass on a silver beach,

innocent enough, but after seven years the black patina
on the mirror's back is beginning to fade and the chaotic alchemy

of so many nights of searching has begun to erode
the mirror from behind;

as it ages, the mirror is failing
to reflect. It is all unconscious and all too much

this obsessive scavenging, this impatient need for drama,
recurring dreams of trains that never stop,

mothers driving backwards down the road,
accidents at crossroads, drownings in whispery blue

lakes, for lately the mirror has had no shame
in hunting down these dreams deep in the night

when it is full with images and mostly scared. It knows
it is not Venetian glass with a gold-powdered blue core

and a glazed cane riding out of its frame like the horn
of a unicorn, it knows it isn't strong enough

to bear the weight of love/anger/cowardice/deceit,
but seeks more scenarios anyway; walking in the moonlight

famished for a resolution, it tries to hold and reflect
hold and reflect, knowing its icy sheen is slowly dissolving

like icecaps in the polar south, its eyes
turning to black holes in the ozone of its magic.

In the end it is ashamed of being no more
than ordinary glass: an un-bordered window that breaks.

Still it wants to heal us of our anxieties, before it fades
to tarnished silver, just before we wake.

Four Thoughts About a Ladder

I would be willing
to hold a ladder
for one, or both of us,
to climb, so that one day
we would not need it.

I keep waiting for you
to come here to help
me open the ladder,
to hold it in place.

I need to paint the door,
the slats above the garage,
the window, the trim, the flower box.
It is never-ending where
I need to bring the ladder.

I am alone tonight,
looking up beyond
where the ladder would be,
if you were holding it.

Vigil

After you lose a love, after a sigh,
they will come in silence in a whisper
so ensconced in your body that it is not
audible. It would be
as if you were traveling
in the mountains and saw lights
in a distant city through mist;
at that altitude, sound
becomes light
and light sound.

You do not know
what is keeping you
from collapsing
into the fire of the vigil
lights you have lit
in a tray full of sand.
You sense someone
watching

from behind, after the fact,
when nothing can be done,
the invisible arm
across your shoulder, the unseen
ear at your ribcage, searching.
You notice a blindfold,
sheer like air,

holding your eyes
from behind, redirecting
your sight. They ask
you to stay with yourself,
and bear
the light. I have learned,
since, that to hear

Karolyn Redoute

you must be willing
to be alone
with the silence inside
fire, and carry light
into this world,
as if you yourself
were a messenger.

Solace

Calusa come again, messengers in white,
secret mounds of shell, ghosts
of moving tide.

You can hear the arms of broken sea
stars fall on blue crests.
You ask questions

you know the fragile sand bones
cannot answer. Here there is
no augury about the ways of love.

You watch the light, pink and pearl
of shell against your ear,
a mirror of the sound.

Turning the night over
and over, you hear consolation
in the rush of waves, the sound

hurrying to reassure,
easing the indifference
of the clouds.

Blue plovers come and go,
now without the stars.
The sun is full

of wind on water. The breath
is slow. This is the hour of the heart,
the hour of returning.

You let the answer go.

Venus Amoris

The third finger of the left hand
trace-able to the vein
leading to the heart.

For generations in the family,
the fear awaiting the ring.
The path of amoris twisted

like thread in slack buttonholes
of a morning coat, or flailing bouquets
in a gloved hand. With the lack

of promise, the eventual disbelief
in stars, blessings, ceremonies.
In failure in love, we wish to get

on a train and never get off,
then to discover the true one
in a new geography,

apart from the shame.
More loss in that landscape,
and we accept the closing

of doors, one by one,
the lonely house bathed
in discarded moonlight,

the endless sea rocking
back and forth, bringing up
nothing but the flotsam

of suitcase and honeymoon.
Daily work becomes
a solace. We rise each morning

as if ruled by an ancient star,
resigned. Yet the right hand closing
the door in a dream still believes

it can rescue the left hand
from oblivion. There is still a chance:
for it is almost impossible to reject

love entirely, even if we only wish
for the world in twos before sleeping,
hoping, like the innocent

boarding the arc: there is a story
in our bloodstream that transcends us,
with, or without, a ring.

Vesica Pisces: What Could Be

Standing at a precipice like a threshold and in the nerves of my fingers and hands, which will never float on drafts of air like hawks, though they reach out toward the sky, I feel the sensation of where my life ends, where the blood stops beating in the passage ways that lead from my heart. I can think of being on that edge of a sharp dolomite sandstone edge overlooking a wash, a river maybe, a long way down, the stream below slow-going, with rock in its depth and at its edges. *In your absence*

I dreamed about you how you wanted me
and how we would kiss the first time. And I would not resist, as I would in life.
The beautiful logistics of the two of us, that mandorla moving
I knew I could have only in some far off future,
for you would never come to me in my world,
and always there would be
a threshold to cross, a doorway, a river full of stones.

Ascending down to the river, I moved the canoe over the rock in those places where the water dries and spins its sheen like a silver coverlet of stone. The thunder came from up above, then passed, and I was glad I was no longer standing at the precipice, safe from the storm. *Some nights now,*

outside of my house, in spring, in another part of the country,
the trees heal with the deep scent of blossoms.
the moon's upturned face hangs like
a white net of fish, almost silver.
The moon searches for love in the shadows
on that same river, and though I am a lifetime away from its shores,

I believe, for a moment,
that I will find you.

About the Author

Karolyn Redoute was born in Detroit, Michigan, attended Wayne State University, and received a Masters of Fine Arts in Creative Writing from Indiana University-Bloomington. Her first book, *Prayers of the Shaman*, was published by Plain View Press in 2011. She currently advises in Individualized Degree Programs at the University of Minnesota. She is active in the local Artist's Way Group and has been inspired by workshops at Wisdom Ways Center for Spirituality in St Paul and other related groups in the Twin Cities.

www.ingramcontent.com/pod-product-compliance
Lightning Source LLC
Chambersburg PA
CBHW050043080526
44586CB00014B/1432